Children's Reference

SCIENCE & TECHNOLOGY

Contents

Matter

Everything around us is made of matter. All objects, living and non-living, which occupy space and have weight, are matter. Matter can be varied in shape and form. It can be hard like stone, soft like cotton, heavy like iron, or light like a feather.

Key facts:

- Some fluids form crystals when they solidify. Crystals are special kinds of solids that have a regular, orderly and repeating pattern of atoms, which form a "crystal lattice." Some fluids solidify to form a single crystal, but most form into several interconnected "polycrystals."

- Ancient Greeks and Indians thought that all matter was made up of the four natural elements: earth, fire, water, and air. The 6th-century Indian philosopher Kanada was the first to suggest that all matter was made up of tiny particles called *Parmanu*, or atoms. However, these theories and discoveries were gradually forgotten over the centuries.

- The modern atomic theory was proposed by the renowned English physicist John Dalton, in 1803. In the latter part of the 20th century, scientists discovered the quark and the gluon. These are the smallest parts of an atom.

M atter can also be a liquid like water or a gas like oxygen. However, there are three basic forms of matter—solid, liquid, and gas. All three states can be changed into one another, by heating or cooling. Solids have a definite shape, volume, or size. Liquids have volume but they do not have a definite shape. They take on the shape of the container that holds them. Gases do not have a fixed shape or volume. They expand and fill the area or container they are put into.

What is matter made of?

Matter is made up of tiny particles called molecules, which can be further broken down into atoms. Atoms are the smallest particles that retain the chemical properties of the particular matter. The atoms of each material differ from those of other materials. Solids are made up of tightly packed atoms, which give them their shape and hardness. Liquids have atoms that are not as tightly packed as in solids, but are closer together than in gases. Gases have atoms that are spread out. Solids and liquids cannot be compressed and fitted into smaller spaces as there is not much space between their atoms. Gases, on the other hand, can be easily compressed as there is plenty of space between their atoms.

▲ **Solid facts**
Solids have a definite shape and volume because their molecules are packed together tightly. The closer the molecules are, the harder the solid. The molecules of cotton are more loosely packed than those of a stone or wood. That is why cotton is softer than the other two.

▶ **Changing shapes**
Pour colored water into beakers of different shapes. You will see the water take up the shape of the particular beaker.

▶ **Forces at play**
The attractive force between liquid molecules is called cohesive force, while the one between a liquid and a solid is called adhesive force. When the cohesive force is stronger than the adhesive force, the surface of the liquid tends to curve inward, as is the case with water drops on a waxy surface or on leaves.

Elements

All matter around us is made up of some basic substances called elements. Elements are substances that occur in nature. These substances cannot be made by combining other substances. The oxygen that we breathe and iron are two examples of elements. Both of these substances can be found naurally.

Compounds and mixtures

Some substances are made by combining two or more elements. Such substances are called compounds. For example, when an object made of iron is exposed to air, chemical changes take place and rust forms on its surface over a period of time. Rust is iron oxide, which is a combination of iron and oxygen. A third group of materials can be made by mixing two or more substances. These are called mixtures. Unlike compounds, mixtures are only formed through physical changes. No chemical changes occur in the substances of a mixture. For example, sugar dissolved in a glass of water is a mixture. On heating this mixture, the water evaporates and sugar remains at the bottom of the glass.

▲ **Breaking bonds**
Tearing a sheet of paper causes only a physical change, as the pieces are still that of paper. Burning a sheet of paper, however, breaks down the bonds that hold the atoms together, changing the chemical nature of paper.

◀ **Filling up**
The molecules of a gas are spread out, as no force keeps them together. They move about in different directions at high speeds and occupy any amount of space they can. That is why even a small amount of gas can fill an entire balloon, no matter what its shape or size.

Physical–chemical changes

Every time energy is added to a paricular substance or taken away from it (e.g. heating or cooling), that substance undergoes some physical changes. A physical change can be defined as one in which the state of the substance changes. However, the chemical properties of the substance remain the same. For example, water contains two parts of hydrogen and one part of oxygen when it is in its liquid state. This chemical composition remains the same even when it is a solid or vapor. This is why water can be turned into ice by cooling it and into water vapor by heating it. Both ice and water vapor can be changed back into water. If adding or taking away energy changes the substance irreversibly, then the change is chemical. For example, if paper is burned it turns into ash and cannot be changed back into its original form.

Atomic structure

Atoms are made up of three parts. They are electrons, neutrons, and protons. The neutrons and protons form the nucleus, or the center of the atom, while the electrons travel around this nucleus. The electron has a negative electric charge and the proton has a positive electric charge. The neutron, however, has no electric charge. The number of electrons, protons, and neutrons in an atom varies according to the type of atom.

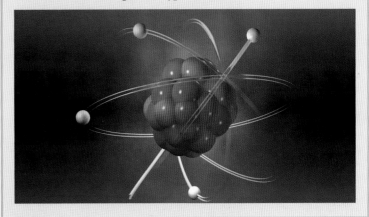

Light

Light is a form of energy that helps us see. It is all around us and is produced by natural and artificial sources. Light sources also produce heat—another form of energy.

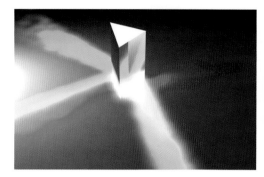

▲ **Dispersing colors**
When light enters a glass prism, it bends. Since each color in white light has a different wavelength, they travel at different speeds. The color with less speed is bent more than the one that travels faster, causing them to be separated. This property is called dispersion.

Key facts:

• When light falls on an object, some of it is scattered around the object, enabling us to see it. This is called "scattering of light." Some light is absorbed by the object and the rest is reflected. The amount of light that is absorbed depends on the nature of the object. Smooth and transparent objects like glass absorb very little, but opaque objects like wood absorb a lot and reflect very little.

• White light can be made by mixing red, green, and blue light in the right proportion. These colors are called primary colors and a wide range of other colors can be produced by varying combinations of them. Unlike colored light, colored paints cannot be added to each other to produce white. While mixing, some colors absorb others and mixing all three together will only produce a blackish-brown color!

• The human eye sees objects with the help of two types of cells—rods and cones. Cones can recognize colors and help form images that are bright and colorful. Rods help in seeing at night and in the dark. They cannot recognize colors, which is why everything appears black or grey at night.

The Sun is the largest natural source of light. The surface temperature of the Sun is more than 6,000° C (11,000° F) and at the center it is nearly 13,000,000° C (23,400,032° F). All this heat makes the surface of the Sun glow brightly. This bright glow is what we see on Earth as sunlight. Other stars also produce light, but they are too far away to light up the Earth. The Moon is another heavenly body that appears to produce light, but in reality it is just reflecting the light of the Sun.

Artificial sources of light include oil lamps, candles, incandescent bulbs, and fluorescent lights. The Sun, stars, lamps, candles, and bulbs are called luminous objects. Objects like trees, buildings, and furniture, which do not produce light, are called non-luminous objects. These can be seen only when light falls onto them and they reflect it.

▼ **Faster than sound**
Light travels at a speed of 186,411 miles/second (300,000 kilometers/second), which is a million times faster than the speed of sound.

Colors in light

Light mostly appears to be white or yellow, but it is actually made up of numerous colors. Isaac Newton discovered that light passing through a glass prism will be broken down into violet, indigo, blue, green, yellow, orange, and red (VIBGYOR). This is best demonstrated by the rainbow. The color of the objects around us is determined by which colors of light they absorb and which ones they reflect. A red object absorbs most of the colors and reflects red. Black objects absorb most colors, to appear dark, while white ones reflect most colors, to appear white.

Seeing light

We can see ourselves in a mirror because light bounces off its surface. Polished metal, water and glass have smooth, shiny surfaces that easily reflect light. Rough surfaces scatter the reflection. Kaleidoscopes and periscopes are excellent examples of how reflecting surfaces can be used in clever ways. In a kaleidoscope, a set of two mirrors is used to create multiple reflections of colored patterns, while in a periscope two glass prisms are used to reflect objects above through the eyepiece below.

Light travels at different speeds in different mediums. While traveling from one transparent medium to another it changes its direction slightly. This bending of light is called refraction. For example, if a pencil is placed in a partially-filled jar of water, we can see that the pencil appears to bend where it enters the water. This happens due to refraction.

Traveling light

Light can travel through empty space, even in a vacuum where there is no air. To the naked eye, light appears to travel in straight lines. Light emitted by a flashlight is an example of this. However, in reality, light travels in waves. It travels only in one direction, but in a way that is similar to ripples in a pond—with continuous crests (peaks) and troughs (valleys). Light is measured by the distance between two consecutive crests, which is its "wavelength" and the height of the crest from the trough, which is its "amplitude" (amount of energy). Each color that makes up white light has a different wavelength.

Shadows

Shadows are formed when light is blocked by an object. All materials that block light even a little can form shadows. This means that even tissue paper and soap bubbles, both of which allow light to pass through them, form shadows because they are not completely transparent. However, solids, like us, form the darkest shadows. This is because we block light completely. The sharpness and the length of a shadow depend on the position of the light source and its distance from the object. A single bright beam of light coming from one direction casts a clear shadow, whereas if light is cast from several beams coming from different directions, there may not be a shadow, or it may be blurred.

◄ Reflecting colors
The kaleidoscope has a transparent compartment with bits of colored glass or paper at one end of the cylinder and a viewing hole at the opposite end. Within the cylinder are two long mirrors that create multiple reflections of the patterns created by the colored bits.

▲ In the candlelight
Like light bulbs, candles are artificial sources of light. They consist of a wick inside a column of solid fuel made of wax. Like all light sources, candles emit heat as well as light.

◄ Skewed vision
In the picture, the line dividing the red and white surfaces seems skewed when seen through the glass of water. This is due to the refraction of light.

◄ Clear image
Reflections on still water are called specular reflections. In specular reflection, light coming from a particular direction is reflected on to a single direction, giving a clear image on the surface of the reflecting medium.

Sound

Sound is a kind of energy that we can hear. Sounds are produced all around us and we hear them without actually trying to do so. This is because the human ear automatically collects sound messages and transmits them to our brain. Sound can travel through air, water, and even solids, but not through a vacuum.

Key facts:

- Ultrasonic sound waves are used to help diagnose problems such as muscular and joint injuries and pain. They are also used to scan a fetus during pregnancy and to monitor its growth.

- When an aircraft flies, it creates waves of air that push against each other and form a barrier. When the aircraft's speed exceeds the speed of sound, the barrier of air is broken, causing a loud noise called a sonic boom.

▼ **Getting an earful**
The sound waves entering a human ear cause the eardrum to vibrate. These vibrations are transmitted into the inner ear, where they are converted into nerve impulses and sent to the brain.

Sounds are produced by quick backward and forward movements, or vibrations, of an object. When an object moves, it disturbs the molecules of air around it and causes them to vibrate. This vibration travels through the air and is heard as sound. The greater the vibration, the louder the sound. As sound travels, the energy of the vibration slowly wears out and the sound fades away.

Properties of sound

Sound, like light, travels in waves. The movement of molecules in sound waves causes alternating patches of tightly bunched molecules, called compressions, and loosely spaced molecules, called rarefactions. These are shown in graphs as wavelike figures with crests and troughs, or ups and downs. Sound is measured by its wavelength, period, amplitude, and frequency.

Wavelength is the distance from one crest or trough to another crest or trough, and this constitutes one cycle of the wave. The time taken for the completion of one cycle is the period of the sound.

▼ **Musical notes**
Sounds produced by musical instruments like a trumpet are usually pleasant. However, if not played well even instruments can produce unpleasant noise.

Amplitude is the height of the wave from trough to crest, meaning the louder the sound, the bigger the amplitude. Frequency is the total number of cycles completed in a second. The greater the number of cycles, the higher the frequency and the pitch. Sound travels fastest in solids. This is because denser mediums are able to transmit vibrations faster through their tightly packed molecules. Sound cannot travel in a vacuum, because in empty space there is no medium to carry sound waves.

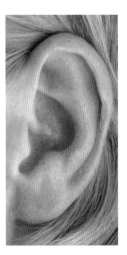

▶ **No barriers**
While sitting next to a person who is listening to music through earphones, one can sometimes faintly hear parts of the music. This is due to diffraction, by which sound waves can bend around obstacles and escape through even the tiniest openings.

Types of sound

There are two types of sounds—those that we can hear and those that we cannot. Sounds we can hear are called audible sounds. The human ear can normally hear sound that ranges between frequencies of 20 hertz and 20,000 hertz. The normal human voice is about 60 hertz. Any sound that is below 20 hertz or above 20,000 hertz is called inaudible sound, or ultrasonic sound. Some animals, like elephants and dogs, can hear ultrasonic sound. Bats can both hear and produce ultrasonic sounds.

Noise and music

Unpleasant sound is called noise. The loud sounds of machinery, aircraft taking off and heavy traffic are created by irregular sound waves that produce disagreeable sounds. Loud sounds are not only disturbing, they can also damage the eardrum and cause partial loss of hearing or deafness. Music is any pleasant sound produced by a singer or a musical instrument. It is created by regular sound waves and consists of a series of high and low frequencies, or pitches, that make up the scale. The musician controls the vibrations so that the correct pitch and amplitude are produced to make specific musical notes.

▼ Keeping the noise out
People who work in factories and on airport runways often wear earmuffs to protect their ears from the noise.

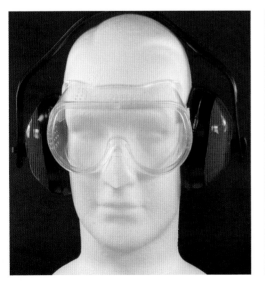

Vocal cords

Human beings produce sound through their voice box, or larynx. Within the voice box are ligaments called vocal cords. Sound is produced when air passes through a slit between the vocal cords and makes them vibrate. Many animals also produce sounds using their vocal cords. However, birds do not have vocal cords and produce sound through a bony ring called the syrinx, which is located in their windpipe.

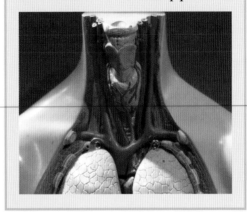

▼ Strong signals
Most male frogs have a pouch, known as the vocal sac, at the bottom of their mouths. A frog usually closes its mouth and nostrils to push air into its vocal cords to produce sound. Some of this air is sent into the vocal sac, which in turn increases the amplitude of the sound produced by the frog's vocal cords.

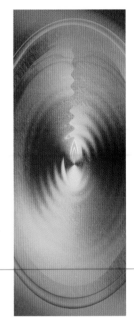

▲ Causing ripples
Like light, sound travels in the form of waves. These waves look like ripples that are caused when a stone is thrown into a body of water.

Heat

Heat is a form of energy. We often convert thermal (heat) energy into other types of energy to help us do work. For example, heat produced by burning coal is changed to steam power, which runs steam engines. Heat energy is constantly in motion—moving from matter with a higher temperature to matter with a lower temperature.

▲ **Reading the mercury levels**
When the bulb of a thermometer is put into a substance, the mercury in it expands and rises up the tube. The level of mercury in the tube gives the temperature of the substance it was put into.

Key facts:

- Energy cannot be destroyed. It is merely converted from one form to another. When the energy in one object or substance reduces, it increases in another.

- Solar heat energy, or radiation, heats the land, oceans and air. The transfer of energy in the atmosphere, over land and on sea, due to differently charged atoms, results in temperature and weather or climate changes.

- The normal temperature of the human body is 37° C (98.6° F). The freezing point of water is 0° C (32° F) and its boiling point is 100° C (212° F).

The largest source of natural heat is the Sun. Fuels like gasoline and wood produce heat. Artificial sources of light, such as a candle or a bulb, also produce heat. Other sources of heat are mechanical machines, such as a saw that cuts wood or a brake that stops a car, and electrical machines, such as a television, radio or food processor. Even our body produces heat when we exercise, work, or simply rub our hands together.

Properties of heat

Solids, liquids, and gases expand when heated. This is because heated matter consists of molecules that are disorganized and in constant motion. A common example of this is the expansion of wooden doors and windows in hot weather. However, all substances do not expand equally. Some solids, liquids, and gases expand faster and to a greater extent than others. Heat can also change the state of matter from solid to liquid or liquid to gas. Lack of heat can also result in reversing the process. The most common example of this is the change of ice into water and water into vapor and vice versa. The temperature at which any matter changes from solid into liquid is called its "melting point" and the point at which it changes from a liquid into a gas is known as its "boiling point." The melting point and boiling point of each substance is different.

◄ **Energetic atoms**
When metal is heated, the atoms in it gain energy and move about rapidly, pushing the neighboring atoms away. This causes the metal to expand.

Measuring heat

We can tell that something is hot by touching it, but to tell us how hot it is we need to use a thermometer. There are several types of thermometer, but the most commonly used types are the clinical thermometer and the laboratory thermometer. Thermometers are slim glass tubes that have a bulb containing mercury at one end.

Marking temperatures

All thermometers have temperature gradings marked on the outside. Clinical thermometers have markings from 35°–42° C (95°–107.6° F). Laboratory thermometers have markings from 0°–100° C (32°–212° F). As heat produced from different sources varies, the calorie is used as the common unit of measurement. A calorie can be defined as the unit of energy that is used to increase the temperature of one gram of water by 1° C (33.8° F).

Transfer of heat

There are three ways in which heat can be passed on, or transferred. They are – conduction, convection, and radiation. Conduction of heat is the direct transfer of heat from a hot solid object to a cold solid object, when they come into contact with each other. The closely packed heated molecules of some solids vibrate vigorously and transfer heat to neighboring molecules when they strike against them, thus gradually passing heat along. Metals are the best conductors, while wood and plastic are good insulators as they do not transfer heat energy. Liquids and gases transfer heat through convection. In this method, cool substances move to warm spots and warm substances move to cool spots in a circular motion. This is best illustrated by cool ocean air moving on to the land at night, while the warm land air expands and rises to move to the sea. Radiation is the method by which heat is transferred in straight lines or rays. The Sun transfers heat in this manner.

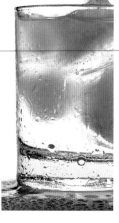

▲ ▶ Good insulators
Wood and plastic are very good insulators. This is because the atoms of wood and plastic are not as tightly packed as those of metals. This slows down the transfer of heat within wood and plastic. This is why houses with wooden floors or windows are able to keep out heat during summer and keep it in during winter. In the same way, plastic food containers are able to seal in or keep out heat.

◀ Up in vapor
The boiling point of water, when water turns into vapor, is 100° C (212° F).

▼ Moving in
When the air over a particular region becomes warm, cooler air descends to take its place. This is best illustrated by cool ocean air moving onto the land at night, while the warm air over the land expands and rises to move over to the sea.

▲ Cold fact
Keep a glass of cold water on a table. After a while, you will see drops of water dripping down the sides of the glass. This is due to the transfer of heat from the warmer table to the glass of cold water. As the heat is transferred, the water becomes warmer, causing the frost on the outside of the glass to melt.

Heat capacity

The rate of heat transfer in each substance is unique. While one gram of water requires 1 calorie of heat to increase its temperature by 1° C (33.8° F), the temperature of one gram of oil is raised by more than 1° by the same amount of heat. This means that the heat capacity of water and oil are not the same. The amount of heat required by each substance to increase the temperature of one kilogram of the substance by 1° C is referred to as its specific heat.

Forces and Motion

Force is the pull or push required to move objects. We use force all the time in our daily lives without even realizing it. Walking, lifting, running, jumping, pulling, pushing, and writing are just some of the activities that require force.

Key facts:

- When two uneven surfaces rub against each other, friction is caused. Friction is a force that opposes the movement of an object by acting on it in the opposite direction. Frictional force usually produces heat.

- The mass of an object is the amount of matter in it. The greater the mass is, the heavier the object, and the heavier the object, the greater the force that needs to be applied to move it. For example, it is easy to move a ball or a puck with an ice-hockey stick, but a lot more force is required to move a rock with the same stick.

- When more than one force acts on an object, the sum of all the forces that are acting on that object is called the "net force." If two or more forces act together on an object in the same direction, the object can be moved faster. If the forces act in opposing directions, they cancel each other out and there is no force on the object.

▶ **Heave ho!**
The bigger an object, the greater its inertia. That is why you have to use a lot more force to push a heavy object compared to one that is lighter.

Objects never move by themselves—they only move when force is applied to them. Similarly, moving objects do not slow down or come to a rest unless an opposing force is applied to stop them. This quality of constant movement or constant rest is called "inertia." A simple example of inertia can be seen in a ball lying on a sports field. As long as no one kicks it, the ball lies in one place without moving. When it is kicked, it begins to move and keeps moving until it hits a goalpost, net, or any other obstacle.

Gravitational force

Gravity is the natural force that is exerted by all objects. This force attracts all close objects to each other. However, as the distance between two objects increases, the gravitational force decreases. Objects with larger mass are affected more by gravitational force, as they have a larger surface area. Similarly, objects with a large mass exert more gravitational force. This is why the Earth's gravitational power is so strong. When an object is at rest, it is motionless because two opposing forces are acting upon it. One is the Earth's downward gravitational pull, and the other is the upward force exerted by the surface on which the object rests.

▲ **Light-weight!**
The feeling of weightlessness on the Moon is caused by the weak gravitational force exerted by it.

It is gravitational force that attracts the Earth to the Sun and the Moon to the Earth. All planets rotate and revolve in their orbits because of gravity. We can feel this force when we try to lift any object. Those with greater mass feel heavier because of the gravitational force that pulls them down. We call this weight. The object also exerts an equal and opposite force. This upward force exerted against the gravitational force is called the apparent weight and is usually equal to the actual weight of the object.

◀ **Moving on up**
Carrying objects up a flight of steps is more difficult than carrying them down. This is because you are going against the force of gravity while climbing up.

Centrifugal and centripetal force

Centripetal and centrifugal forces are opposing forces that act on objects that are moving on circular paths. Objects set in motion normally move in a straight line, unless some other force acts upon them and changes their path. When an object, such as a ball tied to a piece of string, is swung in a circular pattern, a second force acts upon the ball, attracting it to the center of the circle. This is called centripetal force. Simultaneously, an opposing force pushes the ball outward and away from the center, keeping it on its path. This is the centrifugal force.

Velocity, momentum, and acceleration

We measure the speed of movement of any object by its velocity, which is the distance traveled by the object in a certain period of time. It is obvious therefore that still objects do not have velocity.

When any object moves, it is said to have momentum. The amount of momentum in each object depends on how much mass the object has, and how fast that mass is moving. We can find out the momentum of an object by multiplying its mass by its velocity.

When an object begins to move and picks up speed as it travels, the object is said to accelerate. When the same object begins to slow down, it is said to decelerate. In other words, acceleration and deceleration measure the rate of change in the speed of an object. Deceleration can be deliberate, as when you slow down a car, or it can be caused by friction exerted on the object's surface.

▲ **Fighting friction**
Cars used in Formula One racing are specially designed for the purpose. Tyres with fewer treads help to reduce the friction between the car and the race track and achieve maximum speed. The tapered shape of the body and the airfoils, or wings at the front and the rear of the car, help to reduce air friction.

▶ **Forces in action**
As a bungee jumper jumps off a bridge or a cliff, the gravitational force of the Earth pulls the jumper toward it. As the jumper falls at a high speed, the air exerts a frictional force that gradually slows down the jumper, who is then pulled back by the rope.

Forces in daily life

Gravitational force: When a ball is thrown up and comes down to Earth. Cycling up a mountain is difficult, but coming down is easy.
Applied force: Pushing or kicking a ball; lifting weights
Frictional force: Car tyres rubbing against the road; striking a matchstick against the box; rollerskating on a cement road
Magnetic force: Refrigerator magnets; compasses
Centrifugal force: Spin dryers; planets revolving around the Sun
Spring force: Pulling the trigger of a gun to release a bullet; spring-loaded door hinges

Electricity

Electricity is the most commonly used form of energy. It can be easily transferred from one place to another. It can also be just as easily converted into light, heat, or any other form of energy. An electric charge is created by atoms.

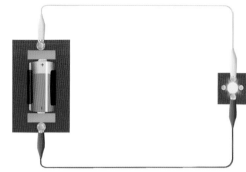

▲ **As simple as that**
A simple electric circuit consists of a battery or generator, which generates current. The current then passes through metal wires to a switch that controls its flow and finally into bulbs and appliances.

Key facts:

- Static electricity is created when we rub against a charged surface, such as a carpet or blanket, and freely floating electrons transfer themselves on to our body. When we touch something that is positively charged, such as a metal doorknob, the extra electrons on our body are attracted to the protons of the metallic object and a tiny spark of electricity is created.

- An electric light bulb contains a very delicate wire called a filament. As the filament is very thin, its atoms collide more often when an electric current is passed through it. Increased atomic activity increases the heat of the wire and makes it glow. At first, the light produced is reddish, and as the heat increases it turns white.

- Air is usually an insulator. However, sometimes, when an object is highly charged, it will pass on electric currents through air or other insulating material in the form of electric arcs. Lightning is an excellent example of this phenomenon.

▶ **Lighting up homes**
Electricity is generated in huge power stations. It is then carried across long distances through electric cables into our homes.

The positively charged protons and the negatively charged electrons in an atom normally balance each other, making the atom neutral. However, although protons stay close to the nucleus of the atom, electrons, being loosely arranged, sometimes move to neighboring atoms and create an imbalance in the charge of the atoms. In such cases, one atom might have more protons and become positively charged, while the other gains more electrons to become negatively charged. This usually happens in materials that are good conductors, such as metal. A material like wood is a good insulator as its electrons do not create a charge. When the electric charge is passed on from one atom to the next in a conductor, an electric current is created.

Electric current

There are two types of electric current—direct current (DC) and alternating current (AC). Direct current always flows in one direction, whereas an alternating current keeps changing its direction. Electric current flows through electric circuits that consist of a good conductor. Copper and silver are the best conductors of electricity, but as silver is very expensive, copper wires are usually used.

Voltage and resistance

The voltage, or strength, of an electric current is determined by how many electrons are sent from one end of the circuit and how many are received at the other end. In other words, there is a difference in pressure between the two ends. This is similar to the flow of water from a tank to a tap. Voltage is measured in volts. In the case of water, difference in height and increase in distance reduces pressure, but in electricity height variations are not important. However, the distance traveled affects the quality of current. Just as water pressure decreases with friction, electric current is prevented from flowing freely because of resistance, which is caused by electrons and atoms colliding with each other. A good conductor has low resistance, while the resistance of a good insulator is high. Shorter and thicker wires have low resistance compared to long thin wires. Resistance is measured in ohms.

Electricity in nature

Lightning is the most commonly known form of natural electricity. Lightning occurs when clouds carrying a negative charge meet positively charged particles on the Earth's surface.

The human body contains a continuous flow of electric current. It is created by neurons, or nerve cells, which convey electric impulses to the brain.

Some kinds of fish, such as the electric eel, can generate an electric shock to defend themselves and to hunt their prey.

◄ Nuclear power
In nuclear power stations, nuclear reaction is used to produce steam that is required to operate the turbines and generators.

◄ Powered by water
In hydroelectric power stations, the force of running water is used to turn the turbines, which in turn operate the generators that produce electricity. Many countries rely on hydro-electric power stations.

Sources of electricity

The two most commonly used sources of electricity are electrolytic cells and large power generators. An electrolytic cell consists of several batteries. These batteries contain chemicals that react with each other and produce energy, which is converted into electricity. Small batteries are also used to produce power to run portable machines like music systems, torches, and clocks. However, batteries and electrolytic cells can only produce small quantities of electricity and we need a lot more to light our homes and offices and run household appliances such as televisions, refrigerators, and dishwashers.

Generating electricity

Power stations produce electricity by various methods. One method involves converting energy generated by water flowing through a dam (hydroelectricity); another method uses heat produced by burning coal (thermal electricity). Windmills (wind power), nuclear reactions (nuclear power), and heat from the Earth's core (geothermal electricity) are also used to generate electricity. This power is then distributed to homes, factories, and offices through a grid of wires that are several thousand miles long.

▶ Not so reliable
Using wind power to generate electricity is very expensive as it requires a large amount of open space. Moreover, wind is unpredictable.

Communication and Satellites

Just as natural satellites such as the Earth and other planets orbit the Sun and the Moon orbits the Earth, several man-made satellites also orbit our planet. These artificial satellites are the lifelines of modern communication devices.

Key facts:

- Satellite constellations are groups of satellites that are meant to serve a common purpose. The Global Positioning System is one such constellation, with six orbital planes consisting of four satellites each.

- *Sputnik 1* was the first satellite ever to be launched into outer space. It was launched on October 4, 1957, to a height of about 150 miles (250 kilometers), by the Soviet Union. The mission was to collect information about the ionosphere. Three months later, the satellite burned up and was destroyed as it re-entered Earth's atmosphere.

- The Hubble Space Telescope was launched in 1990 by NASA to transmit images of outer space to astronomical stations on the Earth. The telescope sent back clear, sharp images of the Universe, which have contributed greatly to our understanding of celestial bodies and events attached to them. Images from the Hubble telescope also showed us that nearly 50 billion galaxies already exist in the Universe, while many new ones are forming.

Satellites are data centers that are equipped to collect and distribute a wide range of information. They receive signals from Earth or other heavenly bodies and send them back to Earth. Satellites help facilitate television and radio broadcasting and assist in studies of the Earth and its atmosphere, as well as other planets and celestial phenomena. They also help in forecasting weather.

Structure of a satellite

Satellites come in different shapes and sizes. The equipment in each satellite varies according to its purpose. Most satellites have instruments for receiving and recording data, images, and commands and for sending recorded information to receiving stations on Earth. All their systems are controlled by a computer. The energy required for a satellite's activities is generated through solar panels that are attached to it.

Satellite orbits

Satellites orbit Earth in a variety of orbit patterns. The three most commonly used orbits are the geostationary, the polar and the inclined orbits. Geostationary satellites appear to be stationary because they are programed and located in such a way that they move at the same speed as the Earth. Therefore, they appear to be immobile and fixed in the same place.

Polar orbit satellites are aligned with the polar regions. These satellites move along the lines of latitude and pass over both poles in each orbit. However, since this orbit is tilted at 90° to the Equator, it passes over different latitudes in each revolution. This orbit is used by satellites that help in mapping, surveying, spying, and weather forecasting.

The inclined orbit is between 0° and 90°. These satellites are only a few hundred miles away from Earth and their movement is synchronized with the Sun's revolution. Satellites can also be classified depending on their height from Earth: high Earth orbit satellites are more than 22,239 miles (35,790 kilometers) above Earth; low Earth orbit satellites are between 124 and 745 miles (200–1,200 kilometers) from Earth, and medium Earth orbit satellites are 870–22,239 miles (1,400–35,790 kilometers) from Earth.

▲ **Weather monitor**
Geostationary satellites are located above the Equator at approximately 22,233 miles (35,780 kilomeres). They often have trouble clearly receiving and sending information to and from the poles, but are useful in making local weather forecasts.

▼ **Communicating across barriers**
A satellite dish uplinks and downlinks signals to and from communication satellites in the form of waves.

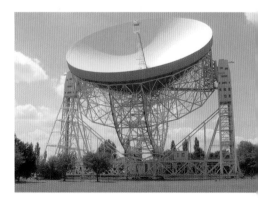

Types and functions of satellites

The three main types of satellites are communication, navigation, and Earth observatory satellites. The most important of these are communication satellites. These satellites have revolutionized the world by facilitating long-distance communication through the receiving and redirecting of radio, television, and telephone signals.

Early communication satellites were just metal-coated balls that could deflect signals they received back to any transmitter that was within their range. However, only very powerful transmitters could receive messages from these satellites. Today, satellites can record information and relay it to specific transmitters, and they provide a cheaper and more effective global communication network than land-based networks.

Communication satellites provide live television broadcasts of events happening in one part of the world to viewers all over the world, and low orbit satellites have revolutionized telephones by making mobile technology possible. Even people living in the remotest places can now communicate easily with the rest of the world. Technology has developed to such an extent that satellites can now send two or three signals simultaneously at different frequencies to different receivers. Efforts are under way to develop satellites that can help the visually impaired to find their way around.

Navigation satellites provide information for land, air, and oceanic navigation. They provide signals to moving objects that help them identify their exact location. These satellites are used for civilian and military purposes and provide three-dimensional views and information about the speed of the vehicle, distance from target, or destination and travel time.

Earth observation satellites are used for military and civilian purposes. They support reconnaissance or spying, surveying, weather forecasting, geodesic studies (mapping and observing the Earth's surface to study the changes in its crust), and monitoring of the atmosphere, oceans, and land masses.

More power to the Sun

Countries such as the United States are working on a new kind of satellite, known as the Solar Power Satellite, or SPS. This high Earth orbit satellite is expected to use microwave power transmission and transmit solar power to receiving antennae on the Earth. This solar power would then be used as an alternative source of energy. The satellite would have an unobstructed view of the Sun and would therefore be able to beam solar power continuously to the Earth. However, the high cost of building and maintaining such a satellite has delayed progress in this field. Efforts are now under way to find cheaper ways of building the satellite.

▲ Signal towers
Radio and mobile phone towers help in good reception of signals.

▼ Finding the way
Today, the Global Positioning System (GPS) is being used worldwide as a major navigational tool in ships, aircraft, and even cars and mine trucks.

◀ Around the Earth
Like satellites, space stations orbit the Earth. The International Space Station's low Earth orbit is about 220 miles (360 kilometers) above the planet's surface. It makes one orbit every 92 minutes, completing 15.7 orbits per day.

ARCTURUS

This edition published in 2011 by Arcturus Publishing Limited
26/27 Bickels Yard, 151-153 Bermondsey Street,
London SE1 3HA

ISBN: 978-1-84858-157-9
CH002016US
Supplier 15, Date 1011, Print run 1201

Designers: Q2A India and Talking Design
Editors: Rebecca Gerlings and Alex Woolf

Printed in China